OBJECTION OVERRULED
Charles S. Mosele

Author: Charles S. Mosele
Address: P. O. Box 20426 Gaborone
Location: Gaborone
Country: Botswana
Contacts: +267 72318074
Email: charlesmosele03@gmail.com
Facebook: Charles S. Mosele – Author

Publisher: Poeticblood Publishers
Email: lameloetopusetso@gmail.com
Contacts: +267 76 969 956

Table of Contents

Acknowledgement

This book would not have been possible without many people's support, encouragement and being challenged to start writing. I want to express my heartfelt gratitude to my publisher, Poeticblood Publishers, who provided the finishing touch in proofreading, giving insightful feedback, clarity and flow to the book. Special thanks to my wife, Dr Minah Mmoni Mosele; despite your thought that you may be 'too conflicted' to proofread, you did it anyway! I am also grateful to my author mentorship 5-day Write A Bestseller Catalyst class for their constructive critiques and friendship. We 'threw' book title ideas at each other and helped one another develop impactful book titles. Lastly, I want to acknowledge the friends whose paths crossed mine as we journeyed through life. Many friends kept asking if I was aware that the encouragement I often gave them had to be packaged in a book format – here it is guys!

Dedication

Dr. Minah Mmoni Mosele, Moratwa & Tlotla
(My beloved wife & kids),
Special thanks to my family for their love and understanding during the long writing process. Ordinarily, a weekend would have provided time for activities like cycling, but writing denied us that chance and you remained patient.

—

Lesego Motlalekgosi (Niece),
You have been the experiment at raising a teenager, and I have fond memories of it.

—

Gaolatlhe Mosele
You made me develop that daring; 'Yes, I can attitude' -Thank you, Mum!

—

Mary, Tebatso, Jane, Nametso, Magdeline, Charity (Siblings) & My In-laws
In being true to the characters that you are, you shaped me into the character that I am.
Patrick & Bernadette Kabasiya
I am grateful that you have been the shift I needed. You have modelled marriage differently and helped me see things more positively.

—

Lot & Gorataone Peolane Motlaleng
Thank you for being yet another couple; you were the last push I needed to shift my thinking beyond being my Pastor. How I wish Mpeo could lay her hands on this book before going to be with the Lord!

—

Bonsai Shongwe,

I knew I wanted to be an author but had no clue what to write about. After two days of your mentorship class, it became crystal clear what my book would be about. What a mentor you are! I am highly grateful, Coach.

. . . .

What a journey it has been. May the good Lord continue to bless you and keep you all for me!

. . . .

In Loving Memory
John Tholonyane Mosele (Dad)
&
Gorataone Peolane Motlaleng

Introduction

Imagine a connection that blossomed not from a mere acquaintance but from years of shared laughter, shared secrets, and shared dreams. This is a tale of such a journey, where friendship is not just the beginning but the very cornerstone of an extraordinary love story. This story celebrates the beauty of turning the pages of friendship into chapters of love. As you embark on the pages of this book, your gaze should be in your backyard, and that is why I want to unfold the secrets and introduce to you the **'F.R.I.E.N.D.S. Love Blueprint,'** where the seeds of companionship are sown, the risks of vulnerability embraced, and the journey towards an enduring romance embarked upon. Join us as we explore the path of recognising the gems that lie within friendship—the backyard, taking those brave steps, and nurturing a love that arises from the familiar grounds of trust. This, dear reader, is the art of turning a friend into a cherished partner—a journey of anxiety, excitement, and endless joy. It's a journey where recognising the immeasurable value of a friend takes centre stage, where the daring risk of revealing one's heart is undertaken, and where patience, as golden as it is, becomes the foundation of a bond that knows no bounds. Dear reader, your associates' views and "objections" that you cannot have your best friend as your spouse are *overruled* here! You can do it, and it is indeed the best thing for you to do!

Chapter 1

The Best Friend Revelation: Anxiety and Excitement

I never considered marriage an option for me. Though I was aware of its existence, it lacked the lustre to lure me into at least investigating what it was all about. I saw marriage as a trap to be avoided by all means. Hence, I even evaded having a girlfriend lest I became interested in getting married. I also believed that my life as a Christian was easier and better without a girlfriend. So instead of having a single friend, labelled girlfriend, thus standing a chance of being influenced into having an interest in ultimately getting married, I had a cluster of ladies I hung out with and the friendships were purely platonic. There was a Church cluster, a cluster for the neighbourhood I lived in, and later on, a varsity campus cluster. Necessarily, it was easier to have such friends to hang out with, share a few jokes and while away time on any given day.

I grew up, and so I changed. The idea of marriage dawned on me when I was a university student. As years passed, the clusters of friends reduced in number to a point where those who remained were the same people at Church as on the University campus, and in the neighbourhood. If not in my neighbourhood, then they would at least be a touch of a button away. With these remnant friends, we had an opportunity to delve deeply into personal issues. I then got to appreciate the warmth of having such friends to the point where I pondered that having a girlfriend was not so bad after all!

· · · ·

IT ALL BEGAN IN OLD Naledi. Old Naledi is nestled in the South East periphery of the city of Gaborone, the Capital of Botswana. It was easier to tell Old Naledi and Gaborone Dam apart because of Old Lobatse Road — the first between-towns tarred road in the Country. That may be why everyone born and bred in Old Naledi in the 1970s and 1980s loved freshwater fish, particularly bream. Old Naledi represented hope against all odds; every in-migrant drawn by the bright light syndrome to the then Town of Gaborone (declared a City in 1986) from rural areas of the Country found refuge there. One just had to have a dream big enough to nudge him/her into quitting rural life to opt for the Town to come and realise their long-held dreams in Old Naledi, the home of fresh breams and fresh dreams.

Old Naledi offered the ideal place for urban life initiates from rural areas. The location presented the warmth of a village and, indeed, the hustle and bustle of a town. What better place could there be to transition, while learning the ropes? The community was warm and welcoming; one just had to know when to leave to avoid overstaying.

Unfortunately, back in the 1980s, those who lived elsewhere in the Town, and to some extent even the rest of the Country, considered residents of Old Naledi as either criminals or upcoming criminals. Well, that had its advantages. During inter-school competitions, pupils from other parts of Gaborone knew better than to try and play monkey tricks on us, the residents, lest they fell on the wrong side of Kasi boys and girls.

Thinking of Old Naledi fills me with nostalgia. This is the place of my birth and upbringing, so I can talk about it until the cows come home because I will always love it. To thrive in this location as a child or an adult, you had to be able to defend your turf before your peers. We avoided timidity for fear that life could become miserable.

The downside to this environment was that there needed to be more married couples around. Further, among the married few, it was rare to see role models that young people could look up to for inspiration and conviction that marriage was a good idea. This could have been because, for most people, Old Naledi was not considered a permanent residence but just a springboard from which to launch life in Town and move on to a permanent place. Hence, even relationships formed there only lasted whilst one was looking for a longer-lasting one. Therefore, to see marriage in a good light, one had to outgrow Old Naledi tendencies and culture to establish, embrace and nurture a new and progressive culture of long-term and lifetime behaviours, actions, tasks and accomplishments. This transition could come through interaction with others from elsewhere and new contacts in training or academic institutions like colleges, universities and workplaces.

• • • •

I ATTENDED MY SENIOR secondary school or high school, as others may call it, at St Joseph's College in Kgale, which is just a stone's throw from Gaborone. It is one of the oldest schools in Botswana, established some ninety-six years ago in 1928. This Catholic boarding school was built on a private farm owned by the Church. The school had boarding facilities, so all students stayed on campus at the time when the school admitted us. We ended up being the last boarding cohort as the school later transitioned into a day school. Hence, at the time when all students were boarding, an affinity existed between students and between students and their teachers. Students and teachers established lifetime friendships here.

Arguing with best friends, mainly, and other classmates over different subject topics taught during lessons on any given day was our unique style of recapping what would have been taught that day. My best friend's name was Lefty. Our friendship started when we were classmates at Ithuteng Primary School in Gaborone. We both were transferred in for our Standard Seven Class. Prior to that, I had attended Tshwaragano Primary School in Old Naledi from Standard One to Standard Six. From Standard Seven, Lefty and I attended a total of four schools together: Ithuteng Primary School, Maikano Community Junior Secondary School (C.J.S.S.) in 1989, where we were the inaugural Form One intake following its construction, founding students if you like, Bokamoso C.J.S.S. in 1990 where we were the second cohort, and St Joseph's College, where we were the last boarding cohort. We became classmates again at St Joseph's College, our senior secondary school. Sometimes, we would allow ourselves time to refer to books and later come together to continue arguing, with one of us playing the devil's advocate and telling the other why their thinking was wrong.

Further, Lefty and I would imagine how tests and/or exam questions were likely to be asked. It was just our way of recapping the day's lessons or how we prepared for the forthcoming tests and examinations; it helped commit materials to memory. This approach to studying carried us through primary school and junior secondary schools. If a stranger were to observe us during such arguments, they could fear that we were close to holding each other by the throat because we would not mince our words in our assertions. The approach paid off because our overall performance was admirable. We often had to argue for a prolonged time, to the point of being emotional, before we could come to a common point when the main objective was to recap the day's lessons.

. . . .

OUR FRIENDSHIP, LEFTY and I, started over a hot argument on whether Christians should have Saturday or Sunday as their day of worship. We were in primary school when the hot debate followed a Religious Education lesson, about the issue of worshipping God. I remember that the following day, we tried to rope in our teacher to give expert advice on the matter, but she refused to or to take sides—as she saw it. We debated the issue over weeks until we agreed to disagree, and following that one-on-one debate, we became friends. I recall an instance at senior secondary school where Lefty had enticed our classmate, a girl called Mmoni, into this debate approach to studying. The duo would sometimes argue, oblivious to the presence of a teacher in the classroom. Quite often, Lefty would rope me into their debates so that, collectively, we could quash Mmoni's viewpoints. After all, we were boys and had to win against a girl.

• • • •

IT WAS COMMON KNOWLEDGE that, at least in the 1990s, senior secondary schools in Botswana formed classes based on an aptitude for science subjects. Essentially, there were three categories: Pure Sciences (Physics, Chemistry and Biology), each of the three as a separate subject; Physical Sciences (where one subject was separate and the other two science subjects were combined); and Combined Sciences (all sciences given the same level of importance without too much detail). My senior secondary school period lasted three years. The three years followed two years at junior secondary or junior high, as others referred to it. In the first of the three years at senior secondary school, Form Three, we were introduced to various subjects. At the end of Form Three, each student chose, with the guidance and approval of teachers, science subjects and optional subjects to add to core subjects and studied those in the remaining two years of Form Four and Form Five. The Pure Sciences group had the heaviest workload of nine subjects, followed by the Physical Sciences and Combined Sciences groups, which had eight and seven subjects, respectively.

I was in the school's only Pure Sciences class, Form Four A. The class was perceived as the *crème de la crème* of St Joseph's College. Hence, being in that class put one miles ahead of his peers regarding self-esteem. Even teachers highly regarded the class. Being in Four A put a lot of pressure on the students, as we had to prove that we were worthy to be a part of the best-performing class in the school. The class was quite argumentative because that accompanied a deeper understanding of concepts. Unfortunately, new teachers to the profession and that class in particular, were not always appreciative of argumentative students. Sometimes, the behaviour was misconstrued as a lack of respect on the part of students.

By the time of our final year at St Joseph's College, we were a pack of four friends with yet another girl. Seally, being the fourth addition to the "debating club" trio, turning it into a debating quartet. The quartet's close-knit friendship grew, and we sometimes spent time together even when there was no subject to debate. At the end of our final year in high school, choices of prom partners for Lefty and I were apparent: Lefty was with Seally, and I was with Mmoni. The prom night was exquisite. We looked like real gentlemen, dapper and all, and the ladies, ready to take on the world! Everything was bathed in elegance for the first time—everybody, everywhere in the school, in formal wear. It was like stepping into a Hollywood movie premiere. The excitement began in our dormitories, which had transformed into bustling beauty salons. There we were, attending to every detail: tuxedos pressed to perfection, gowns flowing like liquid silk, accessories gleaming, hair styled to star quality, and makeup applied with the precision of a Renaissance Artist.

Even the staff, usually in their everyday attire, had undergone a Cinderella-like transformation. They strutted around in outfits so dazzling that, for a moment, we wondered if they had secret lives as runway models.

Making our grand entrance with our prom partners was nothing short of cinematic. Every eye turned our way, jaws dropped, and a wave of admiration swept through the room. We were no longer just 'students'—the word was banished for the evening. We were addressed as ladies and gentlemen, a title upgrade that made us feel like royalty.

Sensitive to the song's beat, we glided across the floor, not missing a step (even if a few toes were occasionally stepped on, it was done with grace). We held and guided the ladies by the hands, ensuring that they did not trip over their own feet since most were not so familiar with walking in stilettos.

And then, the pièce de résistance: a three-course meal that looked straight out of a gourmet magazine. Each dish was more exquisite than the last, a culinary journey that had us feeling like the VIPs at a Michelin-Star restaurant.

The entire night was a whirlwind of elegance, laughter, and a touch of the extraordinary. We didn't just feel special—we felt like stars of a grand, once-in-a-lifetime event.

We completed our Cambridge Overseas School Certificate. Needless to say, the arguing approach to studying paid off, and all four of us obtained First Class! The cherry on top was that Mmoni and I got the same aggregate! Three of us were then accepted into the University of Botswana, where we studied for our Bachelor's Degrees. During that same period, Lefty travelled to neighbouring South Africa to begin his studies at the then University of Bophuthatswana and now North-West University in the City of Mafikeng. Although in a different country, he was not far away as we could reach him in two hours by car, and we often visited each other. There was also the option of travelling to Mafikeng by train, at the time.

The quartet's friendship persisted even at the university level. Because we were no longer classmates and pursued different academic courses, whenever we met, we no longer argued much. Our discussions had more to do with how each of us was trying to make sense of varsity and adult life. Further, since the relationship within the quartet did not have anything to do with romance, each of us sought it elsewhere with other parties. Interestingly, Lefty and Seally had a go at it at one point, but it died before we completed varsity. The ladies beat us to it and were the first ones to have a go at it. Understandably so; they were gorgeous, and boys could not help but marvel at God's divine craftsmanship when they looked at these two ladies. Later, Lefty had a go at romance again at the North West University, where he studied. Only much later, did curiosity get the best of me regarding such relationships.

• • • •

BACK AT ST JOSEPH'S College, all students and a significant number of staff members attended an on-campus church service, also called Mass, every Sunday. For students, it was mandatory. The school Boarding Master, nicknamed Domba, together with the Matron, would travel from one hostel to another, a stick in hand, in search of delinquent boys and girls attempting to skip Mass.

One of the things that made Mass most interesting was the a cappella singing. The singing was simply divine! There was a pretty girl named Graty who represented the kind of girl I could go for if I wanted a girlfriend. Guess what? I was the lead baritone singer, and Graty was the lead soprano singer. Our combination in song was simply fantastic. Sometimes, I wished the hymns could be purely duets so that the rest of the congregation stayed on the side-lines lest they mess up our combination in the melody. The singing could convince everyone that God was excited with the praises and worship that we led. My relationship with Graty was primarily aligned with Church activities, particularly, singing, so there was minimal interaction between us outside the Church. However, we kept in contact even after completing our studies at St Joseph's College.

• • • •

OBJECTION OVERRULED

FOLLOWING THE CAMBRIDGE Overseas School Certificate, individuals could enrol in a national service programme called Tirelo Setshaba. One of its objectives was to promote intercultural exchanges and national unity of Batswana. Annually, there were three intakes or cohorts. The three cohorts started the programme in January, April and August. I was in the January cohort since it was exclusive to matriculants who studied Pure Sciences. Every matriculant would be transported to a village or town different from their own, for job shadowing and stayed there for an entire year as was the requirement. The Botswana Government provided Tirelo Setshaba participants with monthly stipends and free accommodation. Mostly, we stayed with host families who would allocate a room to us as Tirelo Setshaba participants. At the end of the programme, we received a completion certificate and a lump sum divided between a participant and his parents. The completion certificate was one of the requirements to applying for a job in government. I did my Tirelo Setshaba in Maun, so I was one thousand kilometres away from my family, an experience which took a heavy toll on my emotions. I missed my mum terribly.

Apart from staying at the boarding school, I had never travelled and stayed that far away from Mum and Dad, except during school holidays when visiting my maternal grandmother in Molepolole, with whom my siblings and cousins stayed. Visits to my paternal side of the family in Ramotswa were occasional, and they were done during social occasions like weddings and funerals. Boarding at St Joseph's College could not quite be classified as staying away from home as it was less than ten kilometres from Old Naledi. So during weekends, I easily sneaked out of the hostel to visit Mum whenever I missed her. Dad however, would often be out with his friends.

In 1994, the year after we completed our studies at St Joseph's College, there were still no mobile phones in Botswana. The most common way of communication was letter writing. In everyday use, phones were public telephones owned by Botswana Telecommunications Corporation, popularly known as Telecoms at the time and now BTCL. In those days, we would use twenty-five, fifty Thebe, and one Pula coin to make a call.

• • • •

WHEN APPLYING FOR ADMISSION into the University of Botswana, I also applied for accommodation to stay on campus, though I had the option to commute from home. The influence and appreciation of the convenience of having been a boarding student for three years influenced my decision to stay on campus as a University student. There was the benefit of enjoying the transition from adolescence to adulthood with minimal interference from my parents.

The University of Botswana offered me a placement to study for a Bachelor of Arts degree in Social Sciences, and I also secured accommodation on campus. Just like at senior secondary school, the first year was loaded with introductory courses. At the end of the first year, one would then continue with their selected courses after dropping the rest, according to the curriculum guidelines. I chose a double major in Demography and Environmental Science.

• • • •

I WAS GOOD FRIENDS with my former St Joseph's College English Teacher Ms Shay. She was also a church mate. This friendship stood the test of time to the extent that I would sometimes make time to visit her even after I left to study at the University of Botswana. She was a woman of wisdom, and spending time with her always left me wiser!

One given Saturday, while visiting her, our conversation drifted to the possibility of me getting myself a girlfriend. She had become an aunt and confidante, and I felt comfortable telling her stuff I could not discuss with any other adult. I told her I wanted to get a girlfriend who could become my wife. She giggled, as was typical of her. In response, the statement that she made utterly changed the trajectory of my entire life and is what inspired this book. I did not realise it that day, and it took a long time before I reminisced. So, much later, as I pondered the idea of having a girlfriend, introspecting, reflecting and wondering what triggered me, I realised it was my friend's statement on that Saturday. After she had giggled enough, she said, ***"You know what, Charles? Quite often we go out to search for gold in the wilderness when we have left it in our backyard."*** My head and mind went into a whirlwind to unravel the mystery of whether I had a backyard in the first place, and, if I did, what or where was my backyard.

I wondered how I had a backyard and was unaware of it. Could the backyard have been friends from St Joseph's College, with whom I went to the University of Botswana? Could it have been among other friendships founded at the University, or could it have been in the Christian churches? Where was the backyard, and who were its inhabitants or its gems? Even worse, given the extent to which Ms Shay knew and understood me, could it be that she knew who was best suited to be my girlfriend from among her former students who were also my friends, but instead of making my life easier by just saying go for so and so she opted to talk of a metaphorical backyard?

What compounded the problem was that I did not have a hierarchy of friends; they were all equals in terms of friendships. What differed, though, was that, since I had known them for several years, I knew their strengths and weaknesses. I believe they too knew mine. Whenever I had a specific issue to interrogate, I knew who would be the best-suited candidate for that particular issue. For instance, when I was seriously stressed, Mmoni was my go-to person. She always knew what to say to me to get me back on track. Being the active listener that she was, she would ask lots of follow-up questions to appreciate every little detail. There were times when I would offload my issues on her, and I would feel okay thereafter, even when she just listened without uttering a word. It was as though she had some therapeutic listening effect on me.

The Saturday of the onset of the whirlwind about who was in my backyard was a game changer, though it took a while before I acted. Before I recalled the issue of my 'backyard', as introduced by Ms Shay, I never considered, and even excluded myself, from those who could get married in their lifetimes.

• • • •

WHO WOULD HAVE THOUGHT I would act on the prospect of having a girlfriend, and, marry soon after that? I had kept in touch with most of my friends through letters. Graty was one girl who received more letters from me than any other friend. What boy would not want to be in the good books of a pretty girl with such a melodious voice? It happened! Graty and I hit the romance note. I was in my third year, and she was in another tertiary institution. Before starting her tertiary studies, she had left the Catholic Church for a Pentecostal one. Later in the relationship, our discussions often focused on the doctrinal differences between the Catholic Church and the Pentecostal Church. Ultimately, those different viewpoints led to an amicable end to our relationship. However, our friendship stayed the course; every once in a while, we would contact each other to share significant developments in our lives. We completed our studies and started working. Sometime later, I was happy to hear her say she was getting married, and I honoured the invitation to the wedding.

• • • •

CHURCH WAS ONE PLACE that was awash with couples committed to making marriages successful. There is no better place to be a marriage mentee than in the Church. Understandably, marriage is an institution authored by God, and the Church, as the body of Christ, ought to proffer tools to make it successful. Let me also emphasise that it is critical to seek premarital counselling well in advance before tying the knot. When done right, premarital counselling puts you in the rightful place you should be as a fiancé or fiancée. The Church was the place that contributed significantly to my becoming more curious about a well-established relationship in the form of marriage. Blame the Church for the paradigm shift in my thinking!

I continued to uphold my teacher–friend's advice that gold was in my backyard. One word she had said about the gem in my backyard was that though it was still in my backyard, I would have to "search" for it. I interpreted that as saying my first glance in the backyard might be skewed. I needed to be careful and thorough. Boy! Did I find the gem! Who would have thought Mmoni would end up being my cherished wife? The gem I unearthed from my backyard? Our families and friends had always known her as just a good friend of mine.

Chapter 2

Fear of Losing a Cherished Friendship: A Delicate Dance

The revelation and conviction that my best friend, Mmoni, was the gem lingered like a persistent melody. The notion of exploring a romantic relationship within the framework of our enduring friendship both intrigued and terrified me. The journey ahead was veiled in uncertainty, a delicate dance where missteps could jeopardise the harmony we had carefully cultivated over the years.

The fear of losing a cherished friendship cast a shadow over my newfound desire for romantic exploration. Mmoni and I had navigated the waters of companionship with a rhythm that had become second nature. Our debates, arguments, and shared laughter had woven a tapestry of familiarity that felt both comforting and intimidating. Could we risk disrupting this intricate pattern by introducing the complexities of romance?

As I grappled with these thoughts, I found comfort in the memories of our shared history. Our friendship had weathered the storms of adolescence, academic challenges, pursuit of postgraduate studies in different countries, and the transition to adulthood. The foundation we had built seemed resilient, yet the prospect of crossing the boundary into romantic territory introduced an element of vulnerability.

The quartet of friends—Lefty, Mmoni, Seally, and I—had experienced the ebb and flow of life together. We had celebrated triumphs, consoled each other through setbacks, and witnessed the evolution of our individual dreams. We were a familiar sight to each one of us' families. Our parents and siblings knew the other three of the quartet. The prospect of altering the dynamics within this close-knit group was not to be taken lightly.

• • • •

ONE CHRISTMAS EVE, the 24th of December 2001 to be specific, I gathered all the courage to broach the topic with Mmoni. It was usual for me to ask her for a meet-up, when that happened, I would buy snacks like ice-cream for both of us, and we could then sit in some public place and chat the rest of the day away. So, that particular day, we sat at a public park next to the State House, the official residence of the Vice President of Botswana. We sat next to each other on the green metal bench. Fortunately, the benches were placed in a way that each one of them was out of earshot from the other, so even if someone could sit on the next bench, they could not eavesdrop on our conversation except perhaps to hear us laughing or crying depending on the mood. Such a tete-a-tete should not fall on uninvited ears.

The public park was a familiar setting for our debates and discussions. The air was filled with a mixture of anticipation and apprehension as I attempted to articulate the swirling thoughts in my mind. I was heavily laden, with my breathing occasionally catching up speed, to a point where she would occasionally ask if I was okay. "I'm alright. Just that I'm too excited since we have not seen each other for months before today," I would respond. Indeed, it was true that I had missed her dearly, but the main reason for the occasional panting had everything to do with words which were finding it difficult to escape through my mouth into her ears.

"Mmoni," I began cautiously, "have you ever considered the possibility of us being more than just friends?" That question was followed by a long pause on her part and a sigh of relief on my part that finally, the words came out. I felt lighter already! The burden that I had been carrying had finally been offloaded!

Her eyes widened, and for a moment, the familiar twinkle in her gaze seemed to shimmer with a mixture of surprise and curiosity. I could see and feel excitement and shock all at once, and I was unsure which of the two outweighed the other. At the same time, she looked like she had just seen a horror movie. The weight of our shared history hung in the balance, and for a moment, I feared I had unravelled something delicate.

"Charles, we've been through so much together," Mmoni responded, her voice carrying a blend of contemplation and warmth. "But changing the dynamics of our friendship... it's a risk, isn't it? What if it doesn't work out? Are we prepared to lose what we have?"

I countered that with, "What if it worked out? Can we afford to throw away what we know in the depths of our hearts could have been the best thing?"

Another long period of silence ensued. I wondered if she could hear my heart pounding in my chest; if she did, she was too preoccupied with her own pounding heart to say anything about mine.

Her words echoed the very fears that had been haunting my thoughts. The dance between preserving the sanctity of our friendship and exploring the uncharted territory of romance seemed more precarious than ever. We were at the crossroads of a decision that could either deepen our connection or introduce an irreparable rift. I hoped for the latter.

Suddenly, she howled in laughter. I became quite uncomfortable as I had never seen her laugh like that before. Being laughed at makes most of us feel foolish, right? I did not know how to handle that part, so I just sat there. When she was done with the laughter, she said, "I think it is time we parted." I resisted a bit, hoping to get the verdict, whatever it could be. So, I asked when she would respond to my proposal. She said after six months because, she needed to pray about it so that God could guide her ultimate decision. I was disappointed with the response, given the period I was to wait. *The sea is vast; why should I worry about one fish when there is still so much to catch?* I thought. But then again, I asked myself pertinent questions like: what do I stand to lose if I waited six months, mindful that, there was a high chance for success? Besides, she was the specific fish I wanted to hook. I was not looking for just any other fish. So I reluctantly told her she could have her six months.

In the days that followed, our interactions took on a subtle shift. An unspoken tension lingered beneath the surface—a palpable acknowledgement of the uncharted territory we were contemplating. The fear of losing a cherished friendship became a silent companion, a constant reminder of the stakes involved. Fortunately, the New Year of 2002 arrived, and Mmoni had to return to the University of Pretoria, where she studied for her Master's Degree, and I returned to a village called Paje near Serowe, where I was pursuing Officer Cadet Training in the Botswana Defence Force (BDF). The extremely hectic schedule of military training was the therapy I needed. There was minimal time to be preoccupied with girls and their romance issues.

As the quartet of friends continued to navigate the complexities of university life, our individual journeys took unexpected turns. Mmoni and I, once entangled in passionate debates, found ourselves exploring the dynamics of romance. The fear of losing what we held dear lingered, casting a shadow over the tentatively unfurled budding romance.

The delicate dance between friendship and romance required finesse, an understanding that the steps taken had the power to reshape the dynamics forever. Amid this uncertainty, one thing remained constant—the backyard of friendships that had nurtured our growth. The familiarity of shared laughter, the comfort of familiar faces, and the unspoken understanding that transcended words became the compass guiding us through uncharted waters. As the quartet faced the complexities of love, the fear of losing a cherished friendship became a challenge to be confronted.

OBJECTION OVERRULED

The delicate dance continued as a testament to the resilience of bonds forged in the crucible of shared experiences. The journey into the heart of friendship, tinged with the hues of romance, unfolded with a blend of anxiety, excitement, and the unyielding hope that love could indeed find its place without sacrificing what had been cherished for so long. We had ventured into a realm where Mmoni and I met the fear of loss with the courage to discover a love that could withstand the test of time.

Chapter 3

Unveiling the Fear of Incompatibility

Could it be that, more often than not, we fall short of success due to self-imposed limitations? You get convinced because you chose to be; you can deny because you choose denial over conviction. If we started well by establishing a friendship, why can we not nurture it further and take it to a higher level in marriage? Who convinced you that you are incompatible with your best friend? The perception lacks sense: how could you be incompatible when you have been best friends over the years? What was the glue that kept the best friends in a close-knit relationship and could now suddenly lose its adhesive capabilities when the name *marriage* is called? Why do you believe the person who subscribes to that perception? Are you that person's copycat? So many questions!

It is time to consider the alternative. How do you break a false belief that has held you captive over the years? Is it not true that time is ripe to challenge the belief? I want to contend that 'best friend' is a synonym of 'compatible' Hence, we cannot argue that because we are best friends, we are incompatible. The truth is we are best friends because we are compatible!

The tricky part is that when you remove something, you should not allow a void because if you do so, it is easier for what you removed to fall back and occupy its former place. So, replace the false belief of incompatibility with a new and genuine confidence. Nurture the new positive alternative until it becomes integral to your reality.

To a large extent, before friends become best friends, they freely mould each other to be better individuals, the best versions of themselves. The transformation is often unplanned and unintentional as it is a natural reaction to regular interactions and takes compatibility to achieve. When reflecting on the effect a friendship may have had, one might realise that the excellent friend positively impacted them, suggesting that continued association could further develop the other person to be the best version of themselves. Sometimes, it might take a long absence of the other to fully appreciate that their departure may have left a gaping hole or void that proves too difficult to fill. However, it may also be possible to be intentional about assisting a friend to become the best version of themselves when one has identified that the friend needs assistance to harness an undeveloped quality to help them grow as an individual. Where you continue to nurture the friendship and mould each other, you stand a better chance of success in being the beneficiary of your collective hard labour, given the positive impact you each have had on one another, if that option is available. Instead of some more agile guy from nowhere usurping the fruits of your hard labour? Let me also clarify that there are no entitlements here, but it is still okay if your envisioned romance cannot take off; at least you would have cleared the mist. What do you benefit from denying yourself that sustained growth in friendship?

• • • •

IT HELPS TO DRAW STRENGTH and learn from those who have succeeded at what you are thinking of doing or already decided to do. Two couples have made all the difference in my life. I needed to change my mindset and transition to a position where I could look at marriage with admiration and even develop an interest to be a possible candidate to partake in it. These two couples were quite close to me and became my family. To illustrate this, whenever I noticed that my academic work at varsity was under control, I would be inclined to visit friends and relatives during weekends to spend a few hours with them, then later return to campus to sleep. So, during one such weekend outing, I visited Pat and his wife, Berny, the first of the two couples. During that visit, they requested me to house-sit as they intended to go to Serowe over the then forthcoming holiday called the President's Day long weekend. Serowe was Berny's home village, and the couple was to travel there for the long weekend with family. That sounded awesome, so I agreed to house-sit.

What was most exciting about the house-sitting at Pat and Berny's house was that I would not have to join a long queue to eat, as was the case with the varsity refectory. Instead, Berny would overload her refrigerator with delicacies that I did not get to enjoy often. Also, I had a choice of which television channel to watch without consulting anyone, instead of being in a varsity-shared lounge where I had limited to no control over what to watch.

• • • •

IN HOSTELS, WE STAYED in pairs per room as undergraduate students. In the final year at the undergraduate level, few students had the privilege of staying in single rooms. The Friday before the President's Day long weekend for which I agreed to house-sit, I bid my roommate farewell and left for Pat and Berny's house, where I would stay for the four days to follow. The following Monday and Tuesday were declared holidays as well. Upon arrival at Pat and Berny's, they ushered me into their bedroom. I was utterly shocked because I had expected Pat and Berny to give me their spare bedroom. In my frenzy, I mumbled something, trying to enquire why they would want me to sleep in their marital bed. Unfortunately, I do not recall the response they gave at the time, except that part of it was that I should not be too concerned because the linen was clean, and judging by the appearance I could attest to the same, more so that they smelt fresh. They maintained their resolve, so I spent the four nights in that cosy bed.

I made sure that I scrubbed myself quite well each night and that my skin was well moisturised before turning in. On a few occasions, I had overheard people talking about how wonderful staying in a hotel was. On that day, I suspected that sleeping in a hotel was something like what I would experience in the four days that were to follow. I could not wait! The comfort was such that I would wake up the following morning without a persistent alarm ringing in my ear as was the case when I slept in the varsity hostel. I am unsure if dogs ever barked in those four nights. I slept soundly every night, waking up only when my body had had enough rest. The return of the two lovebirds meant the four heavenly nights were over, and everyday life had to resume. The couple dropped me off at the varsity campus and I returned to the campus makeshift bed.

In hindsight, Pat and Berny exemplified an enviable relationship between husband and wife. Spending time with them was great for a young man, and it could also have been great for a young woman, for that matter, to see and feel that marriage is not only doable but can be enjoyed. I have seen them go from being a typical working-class couple that broke even financially to a time when their house was a clear case of comfort, as they had done quite well financially.

I benefited a lot from spending time with Pat and Berny. My background and that of Pat had many similarities, so the advice I received from him resonated well with me because we understood where we came from and what we stood for. I remember one of the nuggets of wisdom he imparted to me: **"You know Charley, my brother, you and I have stayed in these shanty towns all of our childhood lives, so we no longer belong there because we have already done justice to staying there. We ought to be in other places far much better than where we were raised."** He made this statement when I asked him to accompany me to assess a plot that I wanted to buy in order to build a house for my family — in a Self Help Housing Agency (S.H.H.A.) neighbourhood of Extension 25 in Gaborone. Pat rejected both the plot and its location. As I continued searching in different areas of Gaborone, simultaneously seeking his opinion on plots I identified, he repeated his statement so many times that it finally sank in, settled in me and became a game changer for the rest of my life. Pat went further and said that wherever we stay or build our houses, we should drive on tarmac roads until we reach the gates to our yards. "Dusty roads no more, my brother," Pat added.

Finally, Mmoni and I bought a Botswana Housing Corporation (BHC) medium cost house in Gaborone, Block 7. When Pat first saw it his excitement was all over him, as if to say *'Wow! Now my work is done – my mentee has followed advise to the letter'* Pat drove on tarmac right into the Block 7 yard as per his advice.

Interestingly, when he first said those statements, he lived in teachers' quarters, a part of government employees' staff houses offered to his wife Berny, and not the comfortable home he later built for his family. He was a visionary and had decided which direction his life was going, and he wanted the same for me. He knew that the government house his family stayed in was a temporary holding place. Ever since, his statement takes priority whenever I consider buying a property that my family could own and reside in; that I should be able to drive on a tarmac road until I enter the gate to my residence. The statement is testimony to God's Word in **Proverbs 13:20**; New International Version (NIV)

Walk with the wise and become wise, for a companion of fools suffers harm.

I have benefitted significantly from Pat's wisdom as I continued to walk with him. Others would say, "Show me your friends, and I will tell you where you are headed." Better still, others argue that one is the sum average of their five friends. I know these are true because I am a living testimony. I thank God that my friend Pat's impact on me has been profoundly positive.

• • • •

INDEED, THERE WERE many reasons why one would want to spend time with Pat and Berny, as everybody else affectionately called them. Another great motivation to spend time with them over a weekend when I had the chance was because Berny was an excellent cook. The air around this couple was so warm, cosy, and welcoming; you would want to spend as much time with them as much as you possibly could. It is difficult to talk about one of them without mentioning the other. You could see, feel, and touch the love between the two and would want to recreate something like what they had. Secondly, Pat was quite eager to give me some titbits that I needed as a young man, especially regarding the issue of being a provider to one's family. Pat's mentorship, though unsolicited, was excellent; it just flowed.

Berny was a junior secondary school teacher. She was transferred to Nanogang C.J.S.S. Nanogang C.J.S.S. and the University of Botswana are separated only by Jawara Road. Hence, my friends drew closer to me by moving house to Nanogang C.J.S.S. Talk about God, all out to get me, causing a paradigm shift in my thought process and the philosophy I lived by. Without a doubt, Pat and Berny staying close to me greatly benefited me. Pat was my de facto life coach, and Berny was my de facto chef, whom I revered. Could any package beat that?

Whenever I needed a break from the dull varsity refectory food, I could cross the road and indulge in great delicacies at Berny's house. My favourite thing from her kitchen was koeksisters. I am yet to taste koeksisters that are as mouthwatering as those prepared by Berny! Given that I love cooking, it's strange that I failed to get her to teach me how to cook them.

Come to think of it, if I may digress a bit, koeksisters resemble a successful marriage union. Koeksisters are like two sisal rope cords intertwined; they are ordinarily symmetrical and display unity, dependability, and strength in union. Koeksisters are intertwined, just as husband and wife should be. You cannot look at koeksisters and only see one side and not the other. This is the kind of power that a marriage union ought to display; strength found in unity of purpose. If you tried to unwrap one portion of the koeksisters from the other, they both break. Koeksisters look like *magwinya* (fat cakes) except that they are softer, more delicate, much lighter in weight, and more pleasing to the eye and tongue. Further, they give more energy. Koeksisters resemble a marriage whose parties are collectively committed to making it a success. Not only will it be pleasing to those observing such a union, but those in it tend to have inner peace, which they even display on the outside, without a word. Not only are they pleasing to the eye, but they are also inspirational and cheerful, with more energy that tends to positively impact people around them, most of the time unknowingly. They need not say anything; theirs is primarily body language, and one looks at them, sees them, and feels the warmth that embraces them. They could make one recall the Biblical woman with the issue of blood in;

Mark 5:26-27 New International Version (NIV)

26She had suffered a great deal under the care of many doctors and had spent all she had, yet instead of getting better, she grew worse. 27When she heard about Jesus, she came up behind him in the crowd and touched his cloak.

The woman had come into the presence of Jesus, secretly touched the hem of his garment and was healed. That is the effect of coming into the presence of Jesus. Likewise, that was the effect that Pat and Berny had on me. The difference was that Jesus knew that someone had touched the hem of his garment, whereas Pat and Berny did not know what being in their company did for me. Another similarity is that the woman with the Issue of Blood was timid before touching the garment, and after Jesus exposed her, she bore witness to the power that the Lord Jesus had. I, too, have borne witness to the effect of surrounding oneself with people from whom one can glean greatness.

. . . .

THERE WAS YET ANOTHER couple at Nanogang C.J.S.S. that I greatly admired; Lot and his wife, Mpeo. I now have this conviction that God used these couples to transform my perception of marriage and the rest of my life. God used these two couples so that I could observe, learn, touch, and be convinced that even I could marry. Not only that, but I also enjoyed being married because I received the right precepts for an enjoyable marriage from my two couples. Lot and Mpeo just had to finish what Pat and Berny started. The evidence that God put before me was compelling enough to convince me without a shadow of a doubt that marriage was a great thing that I should go into. So, it took two admirable couples to pull this off! The course of my life was changed. What further excuse could I have for not duplicating what I witnessed? This was a rude awakening for me, given that up to the time when I did my second year at the University, I was convinced that marriage was not for me, and I had resolved never to get married. When growing up, observations I had made on marriage unions or such related relationships were quite repulsive. I sought to stay far from all that for the sake of my sanity. That was until I met these two couples who were game changers in my life. However, they have no idea what impact they have had on my life.

I have attempted to impress upon the husbands in these two couples that they have done an excellent job. I doubt if they appreciate the gravity of the impact they have had on my life. Well, I still hope they will take it more seriously one day. If anything, this book should convince them. But I also understand why they may appear not to appreciate the effect they have had fully; they never set out to achieve that or deliberately target me. It just rolled out on its own.

One thing that stood out above everything else in the character of Lot is his humility. He is an interested listener, ever ready to have a hearty and loud laughter. He and his wife Mpeo are similar in this sense. I don't know who between Lot and Mpeo laughed more often and louder than the other. Being the humble man he was, Lot was slow to anger, but whenever he reached the point where he pulled the plug on what he would have considered unacceptable behaviour, there could be no turning back. And the kind of relationship he had with his wife and his children was unique. He would play with the kids like he was just another kid, which was awesome.

It was evident to me that, over and above being husband and wife in love, these two gentlemen and their wives were friends and equals who went all out to support each other. I found that quite remarkable because when you have a friend, your interest is in seeing them succeed at whatever they do, especially something that could be of great benefit to the couple as a collective. Moreover, if you support your friend, it could benefit both of you. That was admirable. The strange part was that they were unaware that they were under observation. I was also unaware that my admiration of them would influence and inspire me to consider having a relationship of that nature. Some common characteristics between myself, Pat and Lot were that, given our humble economic backgrounds, we believed education was our only escape route out of poverty, assuming that the future had no option but to be brighter. This desire to change our circumstances compelled us to give our all to study. Thank God the results were reflective of the concerted efforts invested in studies and affirmed the position that the future had no option but to be brighter.

Getting married to one's best friend deals a crushing blow to the fear of incompatibility. As the journey unfolds, it becomes evident that the true essence of a lasting union lies not in eradicating differences but in embracing and growing through them. The stories of Pat and Berny, Lot and Mpeo, become testimonials to the transformative power of genuine friendship and shared commitment. The fear that once held sway over the prospect of marriage dissipates, making way for the understanding that in the arms of one's best friend, compatibility is not a challenge to be conquered but a beautiful tapestry woven through shared experiences.

The path to enduring love and companionship is not paved by the absence of differences but by the mutual respect, understanding, and continuous growth that thrive within the bonds of friendship, laying the foundation for a marriage that transcends fear and blossoms into a lifelong journey of shared joy and fulfilment.

Chapter 4

Navigating the Fear of Failure/Rejection and Embarrassment

Enhanced operational readiness on any given day is critical to the efficiency and effectiveness of the military. It is the backbone of total army quality. Among others, one of the activities done to ensure operational readiness and efficiency in the BDF was the Inter-Unit Map Reading and Night Navigation Competition, which was held annually. Success in this competition required a combination of both physical and mental endurance within an individual and collectively as a team. I should add that no institution teaches teamwork better than the Army. Inter-Unit Map Reading and Night Navigation Competition is one of the many tools exploited to achieve that.

. . . .

SOMEONE IN THE BOTSWANA Defence Force, specifically, in my unit, Force Ordnance Corps, wanted to see me fail; that was my conviction. How else could they, or anyone, justify nominating me to be captain of an Inter-Unit Map Reading and Night Navigation Competition team when I had never done that before? Consider that against the fact that there were colleagues with a long, continuous history of participating in it annually. Perhaps they wanted me to finally eat humble pie given that my performance was beyond reproach in all other previous assignments including in-service short courses. I imagined someone schemed against me, that I should be humbled by an impossible task. With the energy and high level of commitment to duty that I gave my responsibilities, how could I be treated like that?

I knew that what I had just been assigned to do by management was an order and there was no way out. Despite that, I took it personally and expressed my displeasure to Lieutenant K, who was my senior and had been sent to give me the order. I pointed out to him that I already had a lot of work that needed urgent attention and they should assign other officers who only had little to do. That did not help. I felt humiliated. I asked Lieutenant K whose idea the assignment was so I could see how to engage them, but he refused to give a name or even hint at anyone except to repeatedly say, "Ke barena", meaning, it was the bosses. Deep in my heart, I said, *ke barena*, my foot!

This was atypical behaviour in the military, on my part, since a junior officer was not to ask his senior who sent them when given an order. Orders were as personal to those relaying them, as they were to those who originated them and the institution itself. So it was just me against everyone in management. They truly got me that time. The year was 2004, and I was also of the rank of a Lieutenant. I joined the Botswana Defence Force three years earlier, in 2001, immediately after graduating from the University of Botswana.

At that time, Botswana Defence Force had three formations-departments: The Ground Forces Command, Defence Logistics Command and Air Arm Command. The ground forces affectionately called themselves soldiers on foot. The annual Inter-Unit Map Reading and Night Navigation Competition, for which I was to represent my unit, was used by the soldiers on foot to show why they called themselves soldiers on foot and why they took pride in that. As Logistics Units, we had a long history of failing to get a podium finish in these annual competitions, and it was assumed we lacked the mental fortitude to win competitions that required physical and psychological endurance. That was the accepted culture in the Botswana Defence Force.

Everybody who watched 'soldiers on foot' in action during such operations could tell of their camaraderie; they were admirable and fierce. So, as far as soldiers on foot were concerned, in such competitions, participation by the logistics units was just to tick the box of presence, since embarrassing results were often expected. One could even contend that the logistics units were in it, at best, to watch the competition from within instead of from the outside. Well, one could not blame us because history was testimony to the recurrent success of the soldiers on foot in such competitions against the recurrence of failure by logistics units.

It takes arduous preparation to achieve high-value targets. Operational efficiency and effectiveness of the Army starts at the Defence Logistics Command, so such logisticians took pride and invested the better part of their time in their core mandate, hence their poor performance in physical endurance exercises. Looking at it soberly, Defence Logistics Command and the Ground Forces Command were two sides of a coin, which meant one without the other could make the coin null and void. When Defence Logistics Command carried out its mandate well, there were higher chances of success on the part of Ground Forces Command because the soldiers on foot would have all they required to be most effective in military operations. A desire to win such competitions was a desire to beat soldiers on foot at their core mandate, which could be embarrassing.

Generally, units under the Ground Forces Command dominated in competitions requiring the highest level of mental and physical prowess. Indeed, different units repeatedly won the competition, but what was common among all regular best-performing teams and champions was that they all fell under the Ground Forces Command, except the Special Forces Unit, which was under the Air Arm. So you could understand why I had a fear of failure, why I already felt humiliated when I was told that I was going to be captain of a team representing a logistics unit, and why I suspected that someone in management wanted to get me off my high horse, given the track record of success I had in other activities.

Force Ordnance Corps was commonly referred to by the abbreviation FOC. It was responsible for procuring uniform and camping equipment from external suppliers, followed by distribution within the Army and disposal of the same at the end of their use. Effectively, management had sent a very clear order that participation in the annual Inter-Unit Map Reading and Night Navigation Competition had to be done.

• • • •

I WAS CHOSEN AS THE Team Captain, and I could do nothing about the decision. A day after the emotional turmoil caused by the order, I assembled a team. I had spent the rest of the previous day brainstorming on the best way to move the mountain before me. One essential decision was not to tell the team I had been forced into leading. I felt it was a struggle exclusive to me, and if shared, it could give rise to a rebellious spirit in them, something that the Army abhorred. My Teammates probably thought I had volunteered because, before that assignment, I often voluntarily took them for early morning fitness training before starting our normal day-to-day duties.

During the morning parade, instead of forcing anyone into the team, I asked for volunteers among my colleagues in the unit. Volunteers would be more committed to success, I believed. Each participating team in the Inter-Unit Map Reading and Night Navigation Competition had to have ten members (excluding the captain). I stated what was expected of us in the competition before asking for volunteers. I must have told a great story because the response was excellent, and I ended up with fifteen volunteers, mindful that there was a possibility of sustaining injuries during training for the competition. Hence, instead of returning to the unit to get a replacement who would still be unfit for the competition, I would change from the team reserves, so we had five team reserves.

We had about three months to prepare for the competition, which was a fair period. I collected all the other resources I needed for the competition since we would be away from offices and at an operational site, only to return to offices after the competition. Among other things, the resources included one Land Rover bakkie, maps and prismatic compasses. Talking about the prismatic compass reminds me that this competition did not allow the Global Positioning System (GPS) navigation devices. The idea was that should a soldier find themselves lost or without resources that could make navigation easier, they should still be able to navigate to their target and/or a safer place, depending on what was of material importance. Therefore, the Inter-Unit Map Reading and Night Navigation Competition enhanced every soldier's navigation skills, mental endurance, physical fitness, and the competition was done in the wilderness. Soldiers had to be able to navigate with or without modern-day navigation instruments.

On the third day after Lieutenant K gave me the task, I had my first meeting with my team at our chosen operational site. I informed them that if we wanted and were willing, we could be pioneers of a mindset change and change the accepted culture that units of the Defence Logistics Command could not win a physical endurance competition, attaining something that we had never witnessed anybody achieve before.

My team agreed to heed my call to mindset change and craved to introduce a new culture in the Botswana Defence Force— a culture that realises that the fight in the dog matters and not the dog's size. Pursuing this endeavour may be complex, but how badly one wants the potential benefits should be enough to propel them into action. As we proceeded with our operation, I told my team that the entire competition would take place within a total distance of approximately 30 km, carrying one's rifle, a bottle of water and a light snack. Necessarily, our training ultimately had to condition our bodies to withstand that distance, among other factors. Our consensus was that for our bodies to cope with 30 km on competition day comfortably, our training distance had to exceed 30 km, so we settled for a build-up to a total distance of up to 40 km in our training cycles.

My reason for convincing them to use a longer distance for training cycles was that there could be too much pressure on the day of the competition, which could be overwhelming physically, mentally, and emotionally. Hence, we should not be found wanting in our fitness level if we want to at least come close to winning. So, training harder than the rest and timing the sessions was our only option if we wanted a podium finish.

Fortunately, a few of the team members had previously participated in the competition, though none of them had been captain, nor had they been on a team that got a position that one could write home about. All the same, they had some experiences that the rest of the team could benefit from. So, the day was spent presenting and considering different scenarios, evaluating them, critiquing them, and ultimately agreeing on an execution plan. When the competition was three weeks away, we had covered everything that we set out to cover during the preparation period; including running distances of up to 40 km on any given day. So, our execution plan for training was a success.

Three weeks before the competition, I realised that I was a skilled team builder and an inspiring captain. My team was well-prepared, and I had successfully established a strong Inter-Unit Map Reading and Night Navigation team. I had taken a less-pursued route, and it turned out great; thus, my excitement was over the top. At that point, I was enthusiastic about the success of a well-executed training plan. There was a transformation in how I perceived the competition, and my self-image and perception of my team's chances of success soared. I had done the groundwork! I was highly motivated since my team had become a force to be reckoned with. My team and I had the conviction that we were unbeatable. It was interesting that in our minds, we had already won the competition three weeks before it happened in the field. We encountered a mindset change, and the next move was to change what appeared to be the traditional mindset in the BDF.

We then started night training—a mock competition—so that our preparations could truly reflect the day of the competition. This convinced me that for any high-value project, one has to win it in one's mind before it manifests in the physical.

Since we were sixteen in total, I divided the team into two teams of eight and competed against each other. Ultimately, we assembled the final team for the competition. One thing we believed in was that victory was ours. Thus, a podium finish was our only option. Team members had been conversing with competitor teams under the Ground Forces Command—a reconnaissance mission of sorts. It is vital to have some means of intelligence gathering to measure what you are up against so that corrective measures are taken ahead of time if something is lacking, ensuring combat readiness. My team realised that we were better prepared than them. Inwardly, I was excited with the reconnaissance report they gave. Outwardly, I warned them that what our opponents from the Ground Forces Command said was far from the truth, that they had been lied to so that they could rest on their laurels to ensure that they could be trampled over on the final day. My analysis, interpretation, and caution of the intelligence they gave me annoyed them because they felt fooled by the teams they conversed with about the competition. This helped maintain the fighting and winning spirit I wanted to sustain in them. When the competition was seven days away, other teams went harder on training, suggesting panic and ill-preparedness on their part. We reduced the intensity of our training significantly to allow our muscles to recover in readiness for the final day.

• • • •

THE COMPETITION STARTED in the late afternoon, taking advantage of natural light before dusk to get the teams going. The terrain was characterised by hills, riverbeds and thickets, all of which were to be navigated in the darkness that would quickly befall us. Given the impressive physical condition of all sixteen team members, including myself, we selected the top ten among us. As a result, five team members and I reluctantly took on the role of spectators to cheer the team on.

The exercise's Command and Control area, located at Mmakanke Lands, also served as the starting and ending point. Shockwaves swept over the BDF when the Force Ordnance Corps team was the first to arrive at the finishing point, well ahead of the rest, scooping position one, and subsequently called forward to be recognised as the champion! Prior to that day, we were only known as those responsible for the procurement of military uniforms, camping equipment and nothing else. However, on that day we also became known as the Best Inter-Unit Map Reading and Night Navigation Team in the BDF. In the background, one could hear other teams muttering, "ba diaparo ba winne," meaning soldiers dealing with the procurement of uniform had won, a fact that was too hard for them to swallow. That remarkable achievement remained the defining moment of my career as a military officer, team builder, mindset changer and inspirational leader! My team proudly, loudly and repeatedly shouted, "Morena (Sir), we did it." I was the most important man on the earth's surface at that moment. What an incredible feeling it was!

In that moment of triumph, I remembered Mum and Dad, my number 1 cheerleaders. As far as I can remember, and especially in my teens, they always told me that I always achieved my goals when I was resolutely sold on doing so. So much so that whenever I told them that I had not succeeded at something I did, they would be quick to ask why I was half-hearted about doing it. That day, I believed their collective conviction. I wished they were there to see me walk tall and proudly being celebrated by my colleagues.

We made an indelible mark in the history of the BDF. Nobody could recall a time in their career in the BDF when a logistics unit won first place in the Inter-Unit Map Reading and Night Navigation competition, until that day when my team and I achieved it!

I could not believe that I made it happen! That was truly a dream come true. I had changed not only my mindset as an individual but that of the team and, most importantly, the BDF as well. It was the dawn of a new culture—one in which if one identified what it could take to succeed, calculated the involved risk, strategised and strained forward, success was inevitable, regardless of whether some people had previously tried and failed to succeed at it. This new culture would prove that persistence truly was key. All that was required was a mindset change in the leader.

· · · ·

I WAS THE ENVY OF MANY and felt fantastic. The past is important insofar as it is used as a point of reference, which should be recognised as the barest minimum. In other words, a past achievement, or even past failure for that matter, is the base upon which one stands to achieve more incredible things. You should not allow yourself to perform below your past achievements or fall below your past failures. Instead, strive to surpass them. Your future performance should always be better. When that happens, that is growth. As a person who is still alive, keep growing. If you will, dear reader, you too can grow and achieve what you have never witnessed anybody else achieving. All it takes is you; it takes grit.

Considering Apostle Paul's assertion in his letter to the Philippians, he said;

· · · ·

PHILIPPIANS 3:12-14; The Message (MSG)

12 Not that I have already obtained all this, or have already arrived at my goal, but I press on to take hold of that for which Christ Jesus took hold of me. 13 Brothers and sisters, I do not consider myself yet to have taken hold of it. But one thing I do: Forgetting what is behind and straining toward what is ahead, 14 I press on toward the goal to win the prize for which God has called me heavenward in Christ Jesus.

Your current life is a journey in a new direction. You are alive because you have not yet accomplished everything you were meant to and may even be longing for. We have to be in the habit of forgetting our past successes and past failures when they threaten to fill us with self-importance and/or self-pity. Past achievements and past failures are the same in that both are past; they are behind us, and we are on a relentless course to go forward. So, they should not become distractions or enemies against the progress we aspire to attain. In this context, Paul's forgetting meant a conscious refusal to let his past successes absorb his attention to the point of impeding his progress. Do likewise!

Many people believe that it's impossible to turn a friend, especially a best friend, into a spouse. But it's important to be daring and strive for the extraordinary. Forget about past beliefs and become the living proof and testimony that your average Joe needs! People look up to you for inspiration, just as I looked up to Pat and Lot. Take the bold step of entering into a blissful marriage with your best friend; they will remain your best friend even in marriage. In fact, the intimacy between you and your best friend will reach new heights. So, go for it!

Chapter 5

The Benefits of Marrying a Best Friend

The Psalmist David asserted;

Psalm 37:23-24 New King James (NKJ)

23 The steps of a good man are ordered by the Lord, And He delights in his way. 24 Though he fall, he shall not be utterly cast down; For the Lord upholds him with His hand.

In the intricate dance of life, our preconceived notions are sometimes challenged by the divine choreography that orchestrates our journey. My certainty that marriage was not for me echoed the sentiments of the Psalmist David, who believed that a good man's steps are ordered and established by the Lord. Little did I know that, amid my self-assured convictions, God had designed a path to lead me to a profound revelation about love, companionship, and the unexpected joys of marrying my best friend.

My curiosity, a trait intricately woven into the fabric of my being, constantly scanned my surroundings. This habit was not merely about appreciation but a quest for understanding and extracting value from every encounter. Through this lens, I initially observed the challenges and failures that marred the institution of marriage around me. In response, I had adamantly declared my intention to avoid such complexities.

Yet, life's journey is a dynamic narrative, subject to unforeseen twists and turns. Being dynamic and responsive to situations around us is vital in distinguishing the living from the dead. The dead can no longer change their decisions because they have since lost dynamism. Those who are alive may have previously made significant decisions expected to guide the rest of their lives, but because they are still alive and interact with their surroundings, they may realise that the earlier position lost relevance and thus worth revisiting, and perhaps, subsequently worth overhauling. While I had witnessed the fallibility of marriages, I eventually relinquished the burden of owning other people's failures. In doing so, I opened myself to the possibility that my path could deviate from the trajectory I had once determined because I was still alive!

Let me reiterate that I had, at one point, consciously and definitively decided that marriage was not a chapter in my story. Unbeknownst to me, divine intervention had scripted an alternate narrative for me. The intersection of my life with those of Pat and Berny; and Lot and Mpeo; catalysed a paradigm shift that I had never anticipated. It was a subtle but transformative encounter with the reality that, contrary to my staunch beliefs, marriage could be a beautiful and fulfilling journey that I, too, could pursue.

The remarkable thing about life's twists is that they often lead us to places we never intended to go; by hook or crook, yet those places reveal profound truths and unexpected blessings. In navigating my unique route, I discovered that sometimes God's plan for us unfolds in ways we least expect, and depending on the company we keep, our perspectives on life, love, and marriage can undergo radical transformation. In order to benefit from this dynamism, I had to assume full responsibility for my life.

Remember that the good things and the bad things in our past can be obstacles against our progress. So, one is required to quit blaming one's past in order to embrace and benefit from the here and now. This is matured adulthood. I am responsible for what happens to me now and in the future. Unfortunately, one still has the option to remain childish in their deeds and continue hosting their pity party based on their past. An example of this would be someone saying, "Because my family failed to do a thing or two for me, I shall remain bitter and do nothing about it!" When we allow ourselves to learn positively from our past, the lessons should strengthen us. Yes, we may have fallen, but the Lord shall uphold us with his hand!

So, as we delve deeper into the exploration of *The Benefits of Marrying a Best Friend*, let us reflect on the unpredictable nature of life's script and the divine interventions that can reshape our convictions, leading us to the doorstep of unexpected joy and the profound realisation that, in the arms of a best friend, marriage becomes a journey adorned with unparalleled blessings and immeasurable benefits.

As I embarked on the uncharted territory of marriage, I was greeted by the undeniable radiance of the benefits bestowed upon those who choose to marry their best friends. Profound advantages sprouted from cultivating a marital bond with one's confidant and partner in every aspect of navigating life.

Mutually Open Communication

THE CORNERSTONE OF any enduring relationship, especially within the sacred institution of marriage, is the ability to communicate openly and authentically. Marrying a best friend fosters an environment where communication transcends the mere exchange of words; it becomes a dance of souls, a harmonious symphony of understanding. The comfort born from years of friendship paves the way for conversations free from judgment, where vulnerabilities are shared and understood, nurturing a resilient connection in the face of challenges.

Other-Focused Altruistic Support

THE COMMITMENT TO EACH other's well-being extends beyond mere vows in the marriage union. Marrying a best friend involves a profound sense of philanthropic support, where the success and happiness of the other become paramount. The desire to witness one's spouse triumph in their pursuits becomes a shared goal. This altruism creates a mutual uplifting dynamic, where each partner becomes the most prominent and natural cheerleader in the other's journey, fostering an atmosphere of encouragement, inspiration, and shared victories.

Minimal Surprises, Maximum Understanding

UNLIKE THE UNVEILING of unknown facets often accompanying new relationships, marrying a best friend unveils a canvas painted with strokes of familiarity. The extensive history shared in a genuine, open friendship paves the way for minimal surprises. In the realm of a long-standing companionship, pretenses are ruled out, and authentic selves are embraced. The discoveries about each other have unfolded over time, leading to a marriage built on a foundation of genuine connection. This depth of understanding forms an unshakable bond where the true essence of each partner is known, celebrated, and accepted.

Sustained Joy in Marriage

THE AMALGAMATION OF mutually open communication, other-focused generous support, and a foundation built on deep understanding lays the groundwork for sustained joy in marriage. The laughter shared in the light moments, the strength derived from navigating challenges hand in hand, and the warmth of knowing that your spouse is not just a life partner but a cherished best friend contributes to a joy that transcends fleeting happiness. This joy becomes a constant companion, weathering the seasons of life and evolving into a tapestry of shared experiences woven together by the threads of friendship and love. In marriage, a couple needs something that sustains and holds them together, something to want to continue fighting for, even when the going is tough. Friendship then becomes the thing to fight for above all else! Life's storms hurl themselves everywhere, including in Christian marriages. What determines whether a relationship remains or perishes in the storm is the foundation upon which the relationship is built. When a marriage between best friends is Christ-centred, it stands a fighting chance to endure and remain in victory.

The Reassured Best Choice

IN THE GRAND TAPESTRY of life, the decision to marry one's best friend emerges as the pinnacle of discernment. This chapter celebrates the profound benefits that unfold when spouses are not just life partners but companions who have traversed the landscapes of friendship together. The reassurance that your best friend is also your chosen life partner brings an unparalleled sense of peace and fulfilment, making the journey of marriage a harmonious melody of love, understanding, and sustained joy.

Chapter 6

Prioritising Best Friends in the Search for a Spouse

The decision to pursue marriage is deeply personal and should stem from an intrinsic desire rather than external pressure. While outside influences may introduce the idea, taking ownership of the decision is crucial, ensuring it aligns with personal values and aspirations. Thus, embarking on the journey to find a life partner necessitates thoughtful consideration and introspection.

Understanding the Purpose of Marriage

BEFORE DELVING INTO the search for a spouse, it's imperative to discern one's motivations for seeking marriage. What value does marriage add to one's life? Is there a genuine desire to share life's joys and challenges with a partner? These questions lay the foundation for identifying the qualities and considerations that hold priority in the search for a spouse.

Genesis 2:24 King James Version (KJV)

Therefore shall a man leave his father and his mother, and shall cleave unto his wife: and they shall be one flesh.

Drawing from this scripture in the Book of Genesis, the journey towards marriage involves leaving behind previous dependencies and forming a new union, where two individuals become one. Hence, I pursued marriage guided by my conviction that getting married surpassed the benefits of solitude or companionship with others.

Predetermining Qualities and Considerations

INDIVIDUALS CONTEMPLATING marriage must predetermine the qualities and considerations essential in a potential spouse. These parameters serve as guiding principles, ensuring alignment with personal values and aspirations. Moreover, they facilitate effective communication with prospective partners, fostering clarity and mutual understanding. If the qualities and considerations are not predefined, one can end up saying to themselves that suitable candidates are no longer available in their era when their statement should rather have been: *"I do not yet know what I am looking for!"*

Categorising these qualities can streamline the decision-making process. To share my personal experience, when I was at the searching stage, I had two categories, which were a predetermined checklist against which a potential candidate got weighed: Category 1 comprised of non-negotiable traits that formed the foundation of a compatible relationship in accordance with my values. Conversely, Category 2 encompassed highly desirable attributes that, while not essential, contributed to compatibility and shared fulfilment.

To elaborate further and add meat on the bones—with examples from my personal experience, though not exhaustive—my checklist had the following qualities: Category 1: God-fearing Christian, courteous, capable of challenging and engaging me intellectually, pretty, and good self-image. Category 2: Should be my age and or down to five years younger, have a positive outlook, have post-secondary education, and height should be about my shoulder. These worked well for me and may not necessarily fit anybody else as they are only intended for illustrative purposes. The point is to have what is non-negotiable, and what is negotiable and can be compromised as two distinct categories predetermined before marriage proposals are started.

The Role of Friendship in Marriage

CENTRAL TO THE DISCUSSION is recognising marriage as a union grounded in friendship. While romance adds excitement, is desirable and should be present, the enduring bond of friendship sustains a relationship through life's ups and downs. Shared values, interests, and a foundation of friendship cultivate a deeper connection, fostering mutual understanding and support.

Romantic feelings may fluctuate, but friendship provides stability and resilience, anchoring the relationship during challenging times. Therefore, prioritising a spouse who doubles as a best friend ensures compatibility beyond fleeting emotions, laying the groundwork for a lasting and fulfilling marriage.

Embracing Individual Gifts

ECHOING APOSTLE PAUL'S words in the Book of Corinthians;

1 Corinthians 7:7-8 New King James Version (NKJV)

7For I wish that all men were even as I myself. But each one has his own gift from God, one in this manner and another in that. 8But I say to the unmarried and to the widows: It is good for them if they remain even as I am.

Individuals are encouraged to embrace their unique gifts, whether a calling to remain single or a desire for marriage. Neither gift is better than the other. Understanding one's gift guides the path to follow, emphasising compatibility and shared goals in serving a higher purpose, if marriage is the determined gift.

In conclusion, prioritising best friends in the search for a spouse involves a deliberate and reflective process. By predetermining qualities and considerations, individuals can navigate the complexities of relationships with clarity and purpose. Embracing marriage as a union grounded in friendship ensures compatibility and resilience, fostering a deep and enduring connection that transcends fleeting emotions. Ultimately, the journey towards marriage is a personal exploration guided by shared values, mutual respect, and the desire for lifetime companionship.

Chapter 7

The F.R.I.E.N.D.S. Love Blueprint Revealed

IN THE INTRICATE TAPESTRY of life, where friendships are the threads that bind our days together, there lies a treasure trove of untold stories—stories of bonds that evolve, transform, and reach an intense level. Within the intricate tapestry lies a blueprint—a roadmap to transforming friendship into the profound enduring love that transcends time and circumstance.

This book, *Objection Overruled*, is a tale of such a journey, where friendship is not just the beginning but the cornerstone of an extraordinary love story. Welcome to the world of the '**F.R.I.E.N.D.S. Love Blueprint**', where the seeds of companionship are sown, the risks of vulnerability embraced, and the journey towards an enduring romance embarked upon. Indeed, the journey from companionship to romance is both an art and a science—a delicate dance of vulnerability, trust, and unwavering commitment. Join us as we explore the path of recognising the gems that lie within friendship, taking those brave steps. Yes! Brave you should be, to have your own extraordinary story of love and to nurture the love that arises from the familiar grounds of trust. *Objection Overruled*, dear reader, is the art of turning a friend into a cherished partner—a journey of anxiety, excitement, and endless joy.

The '**F.R.I.E.N.D.S. Love Blueprint**' is the culmination of everything discussed in this book, intended to be your "tour guide" as you embark on this exploration of your backyard with the intent to grab hold of one and the best gem in your backyard! Hold on tight to this blueprint as you and I unpack it. It is a blueprint that teaches the principles for turning a female friend into a wife and achieving a happy marriage. It stands for:

F – Foundation of Friendship

R – Recognise Compatibility

I – Intimate Communication

E – Embrace Risk

N – Nurture the Relationship

D – Deepen Emotional Bonds

S – Supportive Network

Love – Cultivate Love

Foundation of Friendship

AT THE HEART OF THE '**F.R.I.E.N.D.S. Love Blueprint**' lies the foundational principle of friendship. Friendship forms the bedrock upon which lasting relationships are built, fostering trust, mutual respect, and understanding. Within the haven of friendship, true intimacy and emotional connection flourish, paving the way for a love that withstands the test of time.

OBJECTION OVERRULED

Debunking the Friend Zone Myth

THE FRIEND ZONE CONCEPT typically suggests that it becomes challenging or impossible to transition to a romantic relationship when someone is a friend. However, the 'F.R.I.E.N.D.S. Love Blueprint' challenges this notion by highlighting the profound potential within a deep friendship. If this notion is only looked at superficially, it can result in self-imposed denial of what could have been the best decision of a lifetime—a clear case of a good thing standing in the way of a great thing. Imagine if I had convinced myself that Mmoni and I had been friends for far too long to become spouses. I do not even understand what that is supposed to mean. Where would I be? Rather, where would *we* be? Mind you, we had been close friends for nine years, and prior to those nine years, we had attended the same schools for over two years. In the two years, we had no interaction. In fact, she claims that she does not have any recollection of me at Maikano and Bokamoso Junior Secondary Schools, where we attended our Form 1 and Form 2, respectively.

After so many years, instead of seeing our friendship as the elephant in the room that stood against chances of exploring romance, we saw it indeed as what it was: a treasure trove out of which we could draw out lots of value that could last us a lifetime. We discovered a mutual standpoint after I had taken the initiative to unveil this dimension to the friendship. Our friendship served as the fertile ground from which our love eventually blossomed. We defied the constraints of the friend zone. We opted not to own other people's failures, collectively valuing the depth of our connection and the potential for something more.

I once asked Mmoni what her greatest motivation was for accepting my proposal. One of the reasons she gave was that the prospect of her best friend marrying someone else, resulting in her having to ask for that person's permission—if at all possible—to talk to me, not only scared her but was also repulsive. She then concluded that she could never want to put herself in that position when she could keep me as a best friend and, most importantly, her husband. A lot was at stake, she admitted! Convinced, Mmoni decided that the best thing to do was to give me the nod! Ooh, God, and she did!

Recognising the Value of Friendship in Marriage

FRIENDSHIP FORMS THE cornerstone of a successful marriage. The bond between partners should be built on a foundation of trust, mutual respect, and genuine companionship. In my case with Mmoni, our longstanding friendship provided a solid foundation for our eventual marriage. Through shared experiences, laughter, and support, we deeply understood each other's values, dreams, and aspirations. When we agreed to become fiancés, we fully knew, as much as it was humanly possible to know about the other, what we had bargained for and got ourselves into it head-on. Our strength is that we generally dislike being lukewarm about anything; we either do something to the best of our abilities or we do not. Ours is an all-or-nothing approach. That is just who Charles and Mmoni are!

OBJECTION OVERRULED

Delving Deep into Personal Issues

TRUE FRIENDSHIP INVOLVES sharing both the joys and struggles of life. Within the context of turning a female best friend into a wife, delving deep into personal issues is essential for fostering intimacy and emotional connection. If there was anyone who always knew how to get me motivated when I otherwise could have been down, it was Mmoni. Some of the issues we shared were about our academic lives. When I triumphed in my exams, she would know and celebrate with me, and when I received results below my expectations, she would know and provide comfort and hope for a better result in future exams.

Mmoni did not always have to say anything. There were times when only her listening to my rant was the therapy that worked, without saying a word. So, we shared many intimate conversations and supported each other through various challenges. This level of emotional intimacy laid the groundwork for our marriage, where we felt comfortable being vulnerable and shared our innermost thoughts and feelings at a time when we did not even know that the friendship would culminate in marriage.

Long-Term Friendship

MMONI AND I BECAME friends and saw each other through senior secondary school, the University of Botswana, and postgraduate pursuits—the point at which we became fiancés. The duration and stages of life we went through together should speak volumes about the depth of our connection. A long-term friendship allows partners to truly get to know each other at a profound level, transcending superficial attraction. Through the highs and lows of life, we supported each other. This strengthened our bond, and ultimately, we protected the depth of our love for one another.

Clearly, not just any of your friends is your potential spouse. That is why the emphasis lies on the best of friends. Indeed, there may be more than one such close friend. Still, with introspection (thorough backyard searching) relating to why each of them matters and engaging them on various issues of interest and future aspirations, you should be able to draw a list, a shortlist, then pick one and do the dreaded 'ultimate interview'.

Transitioning from Friends to Fiancés

THE TRANSITION FROM friends to fiancés represents a significant milestone in the journey from friendship to marriage. As stated earlier, I had predetermined what could constitute an ideal wife for me, someone to whom I could also become an ideal husband. With that settled, I knew what I sought in unambiguous terms. So, even as I led the transition from best friends to boyfriend–girlfriend, a period of reflection, communication, and emotional growth began. By acknowledging our feelings for each other and taking the courageous step towards a romantic relationship, we embraced the potential for deeper intimacy and connection. This transition was made possible by the firm foundation of friendship we built over nine years, demonstrating the transformative power of genuine companionship. You, too, can pull this off!

In summary, the *Foundation of Friendship* within **the 'F.R.I.E.N.D.S. Love Blueprint'** emphasises the transformative potential of deep friendship in turning a female best friend into a wife. By debunking the friend zone myth, recognising the value of friendship in marriage, delving deep into personal issues, nurturing long-term friendship, and embracing the transition from friends to fiancés, couples can lay the groundwork for a love that defies expectations and stands the test of time. Handle it well, and it will work out for you.

Recognise Compatibility

CENTRAL TO THE BLUEPRINT is recognising compatibility—a deep understanding of each other's personalities, values, and aspirations. By knowing and accepting each other's strengths and weaknesses, couples can navigate the complexities of life with grace and resilience. Compatibility fosters harmony and unity, creating a solid foundation for a fulfilling partnership.

Deep Understanding of Personalities

RECOGNISING COMPATIBILITY begins with a deep understanding of each other's personalities. In the case of Mmoni and me, our nine-year friendship provided ample opportunity to get to know each other genuinely at a profound level. We discovered each other's quirks, preferences, and character traits over time, allowing us to appreciate and accept each other for who we are. This understanding of personalities laid the groundwork for a relationship built on mutual respect and genuine admiration. I cannot suggest that a friendship should have lasted a certain period to qualify for marriage. I want to contend that such a standard is non-existent. Nine years of friendship worked for me, and you must find out what time period works for you. Best wishes as you make your discovery.

Alignment of Values and Beliefs

COMPATIBILITY ALSO involves the alignment of values, beliefs, and life goals. Couples with similar values are better equipped to navigate the complexities of life together and find common ground in decision-making processes. Shared experiences and perspectives reveal aligned values and aspirations, strengthen bonds and lay the foundation for a harmonious partnership. Since backgrounds play an essential role in our values and beliefs, Mmoni and I had opportunities in the latter part of our nine years to meet each other's families during social events such as birthday and graduation ceremonies. These further gave us insight into understanding each other's family makeup over and above what we would have told each other.

Mutual Respect for Differences

WHILE COMPATIBILITY often involves similarities, respecting and embracing differences is essential. In a healthy relationship, partners appreciate each other's unique perspectives and experiences, enriching their connection and fostering personal growth.

When common values have been identified, what turns out to be differences can add value to the relationship. Differences may be harnessed as extra strengths because individuals have unique abilities that can help with problem-solving and decision making. Therefore, whoever between the two is more competent at dealing with an issue should be allowed and supported in its resolution. The decision on who should handle the situation should be informed by competence above gender. This approach acknowledges and celebrates differences because they become a collective strength and benefit the union.

Navigating Life's Challenges Together

TRUE COMPATIBILITY is tested in the face of adversity. Compatible couples can weather life's challenges with resilience and grace, drawing strength from their shared bond and unwavering support for each other. Mmoni and I, having maintained a strong friendship through high school, University, and postgraduate studies, faced various challenges together, strengthening our compatibility and reinforcing our commitment to each other.

OBJECTION OVERRULED

Embracing Growth and Change

AS INDIVIDUALS GROW and evolve, so do their relationships. Compatible couples embrace growth and change, supporting each other's personal and professional development while nurturing their bond. Mmoni and I embarked on a journey from friendship to romance, and embraced the changes and challenges that came with our evolving relationship, growing closer together in the process. In our early days in marriage, we predetermined that if one of us had to relocate to another town or country in pursuit of a career or further studies, two things would happen: One; we would evaluate the offer to determine whether to accept or reject it. If accepted, the other party would come along even if it meant resigning from their job.

On that note, my wife was offered a Doctor of Philosophy (PhD) scholarship to study at the University of Copenhagen in Denmark. As agreed in the formative days of our marriage, we examined the pros and cons of accepting the scholarship. Options to consider were resigning from my job or rejecting the scholarship and continuing with business as usual. At the time, we had never travelled to any country beyond our neighbouring countries. So, the prospect of relocating overseas to launch a new life and gain new experiences became as exciting as it was terrifying. It was an opportunity to further my studies, too. So, I studied Master of Science in Environmental and Resource Management at the University of Southern Denmark in the City of Esbjerg.

Mmoni and I have always been convinced that when we agree to do something together and put our all into it, success has no option but to follow; history is testimony to that. Our marriage deserves every effort to fight for. We agreed then that I would resign from my job. Ultimately, I resigned from the military to join my wife in Denmark eight months after her departure. In those eight months, I had remained in Botswana with our firstborn and only child at the time, Moratwa, who was two years old at my resignation. Her younger brother, Tlotla, was born in Denmark two years after we settled in Copenhagen, Denmark.

Recognise Compatibility within the '**F.R.I.E.N.D.S. Love Blueprint**' emphasises the importance of understanding each other's personalities, values, and aspirations in turning a female best friend into a wife. By deepened understanding of each other's personalities, aligning values and beliefs, respecting differences, navigating life's challenges together, and embracing growth, aspirations and change, couples can build a foundation of compatibility that strengthens their bond and paves the way for a fulfilling and enduring relationship.

Intimate Communication

INTIMATE COMMUNICATION serves as the lifeblood of any successful relationship. Through open, honest dialogue, fears, doubts, and expectations are addressed, fostering a deeper connection and understanding. Intimate communication cultivates a safe space for vulnerability, allowing couples to share their innermost thoughts and feelings without fear of judgment or rejection.

Intimate communication in marriage brings a level of trust that somebody else could quickly label as madness. One of our common traits, Mmoni and I, is that when we love, we do so deeply—no holding back, no regrets. We look at each other right between the eyes when communicating our worst fears. There are no rehearsals before talking; we think as we speak. That open, honest, and intimate talking has carried us this far!

Creating a Safe Space for Vulnerability

INTIMATE COMMUNICATION begins with creating a safe space where partners feel comfortable expressing their true thoughts, feelings, and vulnerabilities. Friendship provides a foundation of trust and mutual respect, easing the process of opening up and sharing intimate aspects of life. A couple creates the ideal conditions for intimate communication by cultivating an environment of acceptance and non-judgment.

Sharing Innermost Thoughts and Feelings

INTIMATE COMMUNICATION involves sharing innermost thoughts, feelings, and desires. Through open and honest dialogue, partners can deepen their emotional connection and better understand each other's needs and wishes. A longstanding and strong friendship over several years allowed us to engage in countless conversations where we shared our hopes, fears, and dreams, strengthening our bond and laying the groundwork for deeper intimacy.

Addressing Fears and Expectations

EFFECTIVE COMMUNICATION also involves addressing fears, doubts, and expectations within the relationship. By openly discussing concerns and setting realistic expectations, couples can navigate potential conflicts and misunderstandings with grace and empathy. In our transition from friends to spouses, Mmoni and I addressed fears and concerns about taking our relationship to the next level, ensuring that we were both on the same page and committed to each other's happiness.

Active Listening and Empathetic Understanding

INTIMATE COMMUNICATION is a two-way street that requires active listening and empathetic understanding. Partners must express themselves openly and listen attentively to each other's needs and concerns, seeking clarity where there is a breakdown in understanding what makes the other tick. As open and honest as the communication might be, it still needs to be done within the confines of love and respect for one another. The audience should only be the concerned couple unless they mutually agreed beforehand that an extra ear is necessary.

Resolving Conflict with Respect and Compassion

CONFLICT IS INEVITABLE in any relationship, but how couples navigate conflict can significantly impact the health and longevity of their partnership. Intimate communication involves resolving conflict with respect, compassion, and a willingness to compromise. Mmoni and I developed a strong foundation of trust and mutual respect and approached conflict resolution with maturity and understanding, prioritising the health and happiness of our relationship above all else.

Times of difference of opinion occasionally arise. Such times show that each person is candid in interpreting the situation. Whereas I may tolerate or ignore anybody else when they say or do something that I consider inappropriate, my approach is different regarding my wife. When I feel wronged by her, I voice out the issue within the shortest possible time, ideally on the same day. Yes, some hours may pass to calm down, but I prefer same-day engagement. Same-day engagement allows dealing with one mistake at a time, to avoid a compilation of errors over time, which could be more challenging.

In summary, *Intimate Communication* within the 'F.R.I.E.N.D.S. Love Blueprint' underscores the importance of open, honest dialogue in turning a female best friend into a wife. By creating a safe space for vulnerability, sharing innermost thoughts and feelings, addressing fears and expectations, practising active listening and empathetic understanding, and resolving conflict with respect and compassion, couples can deepen their emotional connection and foster profound and enduring love.

Embrace Risk

EMBARKING ON THE JOURNEY from friendship to romance requires the courage to embrace vulnerability, risk rejection, and pursue love wholeheartedly. By overcoming fears of rejection and stepping outside the comfort zones, couples can unlock their relationship's full potential, forging a bond that is both profound and enduring.

Courage to Express Feelings

EMBRACING RISK INVOLVES summoning the courage to express one's true feelings and desires, even if there's a possibility of rejection. Sometimes, high-value returns follow in the footsteps of high-risk ventures. This notion gave me the courage to take a leap of faith and put my friendship with Mmoni on the line. This courageous act of vulnerability and faith paved the way for a more profound emotional connection and intimacy we now have.

Vulnerability in the Face of Rejection

EMBRACING RISK ALSO means embracing vulnerability, even in the face of potential rejection. On the day that I made my proposal, I felt rejected because Mmoni laughed heartily in my face and quickly said we should call it a day immediately after. I recall seeing her laughing in that manner for the rest of that day and many others. However, our willingness to be vulnerable and authentic with each other ultimately strengthened our bond and deepened our connection.

Stepping Outside Comfort Zones

TO EMBRACE RISK IN love means to step outside your comfort zone and embrace the unknown. Life is more enjoyable with occasional visits to the unknown. The time for the comfort zone was over, so I stepped out into uncharted territory to explore the possibility of a romantic relationship. It was the best thing that I needed to do. By taking risks and pushing boundaries, Mmoni and I opened ourselves up to new experiences and opportunities for growth.

Trusting in the journey

EMBRACING RISK REQUIRES trusting in the journey and having faith that things will unfold as they are guided. Our trust in each other and the strength of our connection allowed Mmoni and I to persevere through challenges and obstacles as we transitioned from friends to fiancés. This unwavering trust in the journey ultimately led us to a deeper, more meaningful relationship.

Embracing the Unknown

ULTIMATELY, EMBRACING risk in love means embracing the unknown and being open to whatever the future may hold. After my proposal, Mmoni's immediate response was that a six-month cooling-off period to introspect and pray about the issue was necessary. Other things were in order, but I had a problem with the duration. I immediately asked myself what my options were in terms of other friends who were alternative candidates who could take Mmoni's place. Alas, there were none!

I was so smitten that I realised I would have to weather the storm and endure the six-month waiting period. I embraced the unknown, not knowing how it would end. As she wanted it, we launched a period of introspection and prayer. I relinquished any high expectations and allowed the relationship to evolve naturally. By embracing the unknown, we opened ourselves to endless possibilities and allowed our love to flourish unexpectedly.

Guess what? Her birthday was exactly three weeks after the "laughing in my face" day. It was my custom to give her a birthday gift. Since she was in Pretoria and I was in Paje, near Serowe village, I decided to call her, to at least wish her a happy birthday. The excitement in her voice that day was quite unusual, the kind that would make you pause and ask what was happening. Well, she said something like, "Starting today, I am officially your girlfriend."

At that point, I felt like telling the Commander of the B.D.F. that I needed a helicopter to take me to Pretoria to attend to an emergency! As you would recall, I was just an Officer Cadet in the B.D.F. and did not have that option. So, I kept my cool but failed to get a good night's sleep for the following few days. That is why I could never forget her birthday, even if I tried, because it means a lot to me. Three months later, during the Easter long weekend, I just had to make my way to Pretoria. Upon my arrival, I proposed marriage to Mmoni, and we tied the knot eighteen months later, in 2003. Hence, it has been twenty years since we got married.

Embrace Risk within the **'F.R.I.E.N.D.S. Love Blueprint'** emphasises the courage and vulnerability required to pursue love wholeheartedly. By summoning the courage to express feelings, embracing vulnerability in the face of rejection, stepping outside comfort zones, trusting in the journey, and embracing the unknown, couples can forge a profound and enduring bond.

Nurture the Relationship

LOVE MUST BE NURTURED and cared for like a delicate flower. Attention to nurturing the flower should be specific to the need at that point. One time, it may only need water; other times, over and above watering, it may need a specific fertiliser or even shade. Otherwise, if the specific need is not identified and met, the flower wilts, loses its attractiveness, and it may die. Couples must invest time and effort into cultivating their relationship, prioritising quality time, shared experiences, and mutual growth. Couples can ensure that their love continues to blossom and thrive by nurturing the relationship with intentionality and purpose. Money should not act as a proxy on behalf of an absent partner in nurturing the relationship. The nurturing takes the two, is personal and intimate.

Prioritising Quality Time Together

NURTURING THE RELATIONSHIP involves prioritising quality time spent together. Quality time together can include engaging in activities both partners enjoy, such as going on dates, exploring new hobbies, or simply spending quiet evenings at home. Prioritising Quality Time Together may involve teaching each other skills the other may not have. For us, in the first year of our marriage, I taught my spouse how to cycle, a passion I have enjoyed all my life. We later bought bicycles for the whole family, so that we could all collectively delight in the fun. Both parties should deliberately prioritise creating time to spend with one another. Spending as much time as possible together, especially in the early days as fiancés and/or newlyweds, is critical to the health of the 'ever after' as that tends to set the tone for the rest of the relationship.

Shared Experiences and Memories

IN MY THIRD YEAR AT the university, I spent three months at a driving school and acquired my driver's licence. From the time I got the licence until Mmoni and I got married three years later, I only had little driving experience. However, when we bid our families goodbye to go on our seven-day honeymoon at Mount Amanzi Holiday Resort in Hartbeespoort, South Africa, my mother-in-law asked me one question: "Do you have a driver's licence?" I answered in the affirmative and of course, she handed me her car keys. I was dumbfounded! Mmoni and I intended to board an Intercape bus from Gaborone to Centurion, Pretoria in South Africa, then get a South African friend, my wife's best friend, Thuti—who was also the best lady at our wedding—to collect us from Centurion and drive us to Hartbeespoort. Thuti had returned to South Africa a few days after our wedding.

I was denied the chance to explain that though I had the licence, I lacked driving experience, especially since it involved driving in South Africa. But then again, the soldier in me recalled my Officer Cadet days when we trained in the military. In those days, when one of us had a daunting task ahead of them, the rest of the team would cheer and urge him, chanting, "tsenya pelo ya tau, skwata," essentially suggesting that to a lion, every animal is a meal; therefore, the size of the meal did not matter. When challenged, one just had to behave like one who had traded one's heart for that of a lion. The reaction, attitude and behaviour were a good measure of the extent to which a military officer had grasped what he was taught as an Officer Cadet. What soldier would show weakness as to tell their mother-in-law that they were too chicken to drive in South Africa? I accepted the challenge that came with the car keys! Driving to South Africa that Friday is one memory that still makes us laugh today because only my wife and I knew the pressure I was in.

Creating shared experiences and memories is essential for nurturing a relationship. Creating new memories together reinforced our bond and deepened our connection.

Mutual Growth and Development

NURTURING THE RELATIONSHIP also involves supporting each other's personal growth and development. My wife and I have supported each other through various milestones and challenges, as illustrated in multiple chapters of this book, cheering each other on as we pursued our dreams and aspirations. By fostering an environment of mutual growth and encouragement, we strengthened our bond and created a partnership built on empowerment and support. We are each other's star cheerleaders.

Effective Communication and Conflict Resolution

EFFECTIVE COMMUNICATION is crucial for nurturing a healthy relationship. Mmoni and I prioritise open and honest communication in addressing any issue or concern with respect and empathy. By practising active listening and constructive feedback, we navigate conflicts and misunderstandings gracefully, strengthening our connection and fostering mutual understanding. Misunderstandings are inevitable in any healthy relationship, and effective communication is vital in dealing with them.

Cultivating Trust and Security

NURTURING THE RELATIONSHIP involves cultivating trust and security within the partnership. Diligence in building a foundation of trust and mutual respect, honouring commitments to each other and prioritising transparency and honesty are critical in cultivating trust and security. Creating a safe and supportive environment fosters a sense of security and stability that allows love to thrive.

In summary, *Nurture the Relationship* within the '**F.R.I.E.N.D.S. Love Blueprint**' emphasises the importance of investing time and effort into cultivating a strong and healthy partnership. By prioritising quality time together, creating shared experiences and memories, supporting mutual growth and development, practising effective communication and conflict resolution, and cultivating trust and security, couples can nurture an enduring and transformative love.

Deepen Emotional Bonds

EMOTIONAL BONDS ARE the lifeblood of a strong and healthy relationship. By deepening emotional intimacy and building trust over time, couples can create a strong foundation for lasting love. Through shared experiences, vulnerability, and mutual support, couples can forge a bond that transcends the superficial and stands the test of time.

Sharing Vulnerabilities and Emotions

DEEPENING EMOTIONAL bonds involves sharing vulnerabilities and emotions with one another. This sharing brings a deeper understanding of each other's innermost thoughts and feelings. By sharing their fears, hopes, and dreams, a couple strengthens their emotional connection and reinforces their bond of trust.

Empathetic Understanding and Support

EMPATHETIC UNDERSTANDING and support are essential for deepening emotional bonds. Mmoni and I offered each other unwavering support and compassion, providing a safe space for one another to express ourselves without fear of judgment. We validated each other's experiences and strengthened our emotional connection by demonstrating empathy and understanding.

Navigating Life's Challenges Together

FACING LIFE'S CHALLENGES together is a powerful way to deepen emotional bonds. A couple strengthens their bond and solidifies their commitment by standing by each other's side during difficult times. Trying times offer an opportunity to truly appreciate that they are securely anchored through their spouse, recognising that the two have become one.

. . . .

Honouring Each Other's Feelings and Needs

DEEPENING EMOTIONAL bonds involves honouring each other's feelings and needs with respect and care. By validating each other's experiences and prioritising mutual understanding, a couple deepens their emotional connection and cultivates a sense of security.

Celebrating Shared Moments of Joy and Success

CELEBRATING SHARED moments of joy and success is essential for deepening emotional bonds. It is important to take pleasure in each other's achievements and milestones, celebrating together life's triumphs. By sharing in each other's happiness and supporting one another's accomplishments, a couple strengthens their bond and creates lasting memories together.

On my Officer Cadet Commissioning Day – the military version of a graduation ceremony, as Officer Cadets we were encouraged to invite members of our families to come and witness the end of the arduous one-year journey of military training. We had two events on that day: the Commissioning Parade and a Dinner hosted by the Commander in our honour. My mum, siblings, two cousins and Mmoni attended the Commissioning Parade. I was in the company of my elder brother Nametso and fiancée Mmoni for the Commissioning Dinner since we were only allowed two guests. Let me point out that my family still did not know that Mmoni had been promoted to fiancée at that point. To them, she was still merely my best friend. Mind you, she had to travel from Pretoria to attend the ceremony, as it was important for us to share this great milestone and achievement together.

Deepen Emotional Bonds within the '**F.R.I.E.N.D.S. Love Blueprint**' emphasises the importance of building trust, sharing vulnerabilities and emotions, offering empathetic understanding and support, navigating life's challenges together, honouring each other's feelings and needs, and celebrating shared moments of joy and success. Couples can deepen their emotional bond and create a profound and enduring love; and foster a solid and intimate connection.

Supportive Network

NO RELATIONSHIP EXISTS in isolation. A supportive network of friends and family is crucial in nurturing and sustaining love. By surrounding themselves with positive influences and a robust support system, couples can weather life's challenges with grace and resilience, certain they are not alone in their journey. Given the extent to which the *working class* can barely make time and focus on building inter-couple relationships, it helps tremendously to have couple outings so that a conducive environment is available for couples to spend time, learn and grow together in the support network.

Friends and Family

A SUPPORTIVE NETWORK includes friends and family who offer encouragement, guidance, and love. Having friends and family with the same values goes a long way in giving emotional support and advice to a couple. Love, emotional support and guidance are mostly unsolicited in this context. Hence, they may flow with an ongoing conversation, thus not pressuring any couple to do as suggested.

A supportive network may yield great results in discussing pertinent issues since it may provide an informal and more relaxed atmosphere, voluntary counselling, and voluntary acceptance of advice. Friends and family are pillars of strength, giving reassurance and perspective during joyful and challenging times.

OBJECTION OVERRULED

Shared Values and Beliefs

A SUPPORTIVE NETWORK shares common values and beliefs aligning with the couple's goals and aspirations. Therefore, a couple should be sensitive to the values and beliefs held by people in their supportive network. Since it cannot be just anyone or any couple, the cohesion should be based on shared values and beliefs. These individuals play an integral role in nurturing love and fostering a sense of belonging and connection.

Emotional and Practical Support

SUPPORTIVE NETWORKS offer emotional and practical support to couples as they navigate life's challenges. Mmoni and I have always treasured holiday treats that involved other couples. These have always been a lot easier to organise in church settings where a few couples would agree to travel on a four-day or so holiday enjoying each other's company. Such trips have an environment that has proven itself conducive to emotional and practical support. Couples learn from each other and return from the journey refreshed, with a strengthened bond, and a reinforced commitment to each other and between couples.

Non-Judgmental Listening Ear

A SUPPORTIVE NETWORK provides a non-judgmental listening ear, allowing couples to express themselves freely without fear of criticism or condemnation. This non-judgmental support fosters trust and intimacy within the relationship, empowering the couple to navigate challenges with confidence and resilience.

Celebration of Love and Milestones

A SUPPORTIVE NETWORK celebrates love and milestones with couples, sharing their joy and happiness. It is great to have a supportive network bound by love above all other things, like being kinsmen. Joy prevails within such a network. This is even greater when the 'go-to' people in the network are married couples themselves. Significant moments like anniversaries and birthdays are marked together. These celebrations reinforce the strength of their bond and remind them of the love and support surrounding them.

In summary, *Supportive Network* within the '**F.R.I.E.N.D.S. Love Blueprint**' emphasises the importance of surrounding oneself with positive influences and a robust support system. By cultivating relationships with friends and family who share common values and beliefs, offering emotional and practical support, providing a non-judgmental listening ear, and celebrating love and milestones, couples can strengthen their bond and nurture a relationship that thrives amidst life's ups and downs.

Cultivate Love

AT THE CORE OF THE '**F.R.I.E.N.D.S. Love Blueprint**' lies the cultivation of love - a deep, enduring, and unwavering love. By prioritising a deep / or enduring friendship, embracing vulnerability, and nurturing the relationship with intention and purpose, couples can create a profound and transformative love. Couples can unlock the true potential of their relationship through the conscious cultivation of love, forging a bond that lasts a lifetime and bringing out the best in each individual.

In essence, the '**F.R.I.E.N.D.S. Love Blueprint**' is not merely a set of principles but a guidebook for transforming friendship into a love that defies expectations and transcends the ordinary. It is a roadmap to navigating the complexities of relationships with grace, authenticity, and unwavering commitment - a journey worth embarking upon, hand-in-hand, with the one who shares your heart and soul.

Prioritising Friendship

CULTIVATING LOVE BEGINS with prioritising the foundation of friendship. It is essential to recognise the importance of maintaining a solid friendship as the cornerstone of the relationship. The couple shares laughter, secrets, and dreams, nurturing the bond that initially brought them together and strengthening the connection.

Embracing Vulnerability

CULTIVATING LOVE INVOLVES embracing vulnerability and opening one's heart to the other person. The couple should be willing to share their deepest fears, hopes, and desires, creating a space of trust and intimacy where they can be authentic. By allowing themselves to be vulnerable, they deepen their emotional connection and foster a sense of closeness and understanding.

Nurturing Affection and Romance

CULTIVATING LOVE REQUIRES nurturing affection and romance within the relationship. A couple makes time to express their love and appreciation for each other through gestures of affection, thoughtful surprises, and meaningful gestures. Both of them need to be appreciated as they continue to have that feel-good effect on each other. They prioritise romantic moments together, repeatedly keeping the flame of passion alive and reigniting their love.

Communicating with Transparency

CULTIVATING LOVE INVOLVES communicating with transparency and honesty. Open and honest dialogue, sharing thoughts, feelings, and concerns with each other openly, is critical to the excellent health of the relationship. Any arising issues or conflicts are dealt with respectfully and compassionately, working together to find solutions and strengthening bonds. When one has an idea intended to benefit the relationship and does not know how the other might feel about it, then there is a need to lay it down in a transparent manner before it is applied.

Investing in Growth and Development

CULTIVATING LOVE MEANS investing in personal and relational growth and development. Husband and wife must support each other's aspirations and dreams, encourage personal growth, and celebrate each other's achievements. They prioritise mutual growth within the relationship, continuously striving to deepen their connection and evolve as individuals and partners.

Practicing Gratitude and Appreciation

CULTIVATING LOVE INVOLVES practising gratitude and appreciation for each other. Husband and wife regularly express gratitude for their love, support, and companionship, acknowledging their role in each other's lives. They celebrate the small moments and cherish the memories they create together, cultivating a sense of joy and appreciation that sustains their love.

In summary, *Cultivate Love* within the '**F.R.I.E.N.D.S. Love Blueprint**' emphasises the intentional effort and commitment required to nurture a deep and enduring connection. By prioritising friendship, embracing vulnerability, nurturing affection and romance, communicating with transparency, investing in growth and development, and practising gratitude and appreciation, couples can cultivate a profound and transformative love. Through this cultivation, couples enrich their lives and strengthen their bond for years to come, and challenge each other to be the best versions of themselves both as individuals and collectively as a couple. This undertaking encourages each individual to have an *"I can do better than the last time"* attitude in being other-focussed. Joy is sustained when this attitude is adopted and balanced between the two individuals in the relationship.

Chapter 8

Discovering Higher Levels of Joy in Marriage

Since marrying my best friend, my life has undergone a remarkable transformation. The decision to exchange vows with someone with whom I shared years of laughter, secrets, and dreams has had a profound positive impact, surpassing any previous notions of happiness in traditional relationships.

Post-Marriage Experiences

IN THE AFTERGLOW OF the wedding, I immerse myself in a world of newfound bliss and contentment. Every moment spent with my best friend-turned-wife is infused with a sense of deep connection and fulfilment, unlike anything I have experienced before. From the simplest of gestures to the grandest of adventures, our shared journey is marked by an unparalleled level of joy that transcends the boundaries of ordinary relationships.

Deeper Joy and Connection

WHAT SETS OUR MARRIAGE apart is the profound depth of joy and connection discovered with my best friend. Unlike the fleeting excitement of initial romance, our bond grows stronger with time. Our marriage is anchored in a friendship that has weathered the storms of life, fostering unparalleled intimacy and understanding. In each other's arms, we find solace, companionship, and unwavering support—a love that knows no bounds.

Ease of Transparency

TRANSPARENCY IS SECOND nature in our marriage, thanks to the foundation of trust and familiarity built as friends. We share our deepest thoughts, fears, and vulnerabilities without hesitation. Marrying my best friend has made it effortless to be open and honest with each other, strengthening our bond and fostering a liberating and profound sense of intimacy.

Understanding of Pasts, Values and Beliefs

HAVING A CLEAR UNDERSTANDING of each other's pasts, values and beliefs has been instrumental in shaping the foundation of our marriage. Through years of friendship, we witnessed each other's triumphs and challenges, joys and sorrows, which have shaped a deep appreciation and acceptance of each other's journey. This mutual understanding is the bedrock of our relationship, allowing us to navigate life's complexities with empathy, compassion, and unwavering support.

In summary, marrying my best friend has brought me unparalleled joy and fulfilment in marriage. Our union is characterised by a deep sense of connection, transparency, and mutual understanding, setting it apart from traditional relationships. Through the shared experiences of laughter, secrets, and dreams, we have discovered a profound, enduring, and transformative love.

The pages of this book serve as a testament to the power of turning a best friend into a cherished life partner. It is a journey of friendship, love, and transformation, from the seeds of companionship sown in shared laughter and shared dreams, to the blossoming of a deep and enduring romance.

As you reflect on this growth, remember the invaluable lessons learned along the way. Appreciate the beauty of prioritising friendship as the foundation of a lasting relationship and the profound joy and fulfilment that can be found in marrying someone who knows and accepts us for who we truly are. Sustained happiness in marriage is not just a dream but a tangible reality, achievable through intentional effort and commitment.

But perhaps the most compelling message is the idea that love—deep, enduring, transformative love—can be found within the familiar territory of existing friendships—the *backyard*! Just as valuable treasures are often discovered in the most unexpected places, so too can valuable relationships be found within the circles of friends we already hold dear.

As we close this book, let us celebrate my journey and reflect on our relationships. Consider the possibility of finding love within your circle of friends, recognising the potential for growth, joy, and fulfilment within these cherished connections. Remember that true happiness in marriage is not just a fleeting moment but a lifelong journey that begins with friendship, nurtured with love, and sustained with unwavering commitment and the fear of God!

As you reflect on my story and the principles outlined in the **'F.R.I.E.N.D.S. Love Blueprint'**, may you find inspiration and guidance for *your* relationships. You can cultivate enduring, transformative, and deeply fulfilling relationships by prioritising friendship, embracing vulnerability, and nurturing your connections with intention and purpose. So, dear reader, as you embark on your journey of love and discovery, keep the lessons of the '**F.R.I.E.N.D.S. Love Blueprint**' close to your heart, knowing that with patience, courage, and unwavering commitment, you can find joy and fulfilment in the bonds you share with those closest to you.

My wish is for you to find inspiration in my story. Please, prioritise the bonds of friendship and embrace the possibility of finding love within the familiar territory of existing friendships. Seek sustained joy and love in marriage. Ultimately, these cherished connections enrich our lives and fill our hearts with the deepest joys. Above all, may you invite and be guided by our Heavenly Father in your search.

Your gold is in your backyard, yearning for you. It doesn't have a mouth to draw your attention, but when you have unearthed it, it shall shine in your palms, causing you to beam with a smile like you never did before. Just unearth it, dear reader! This book, *Objection Overruled*, is my instalment to help you overrule objections and crack the love code into an enduring and blissful marriage!